NORMAN ROCKWELL

Engagement Book & Calendar 1981

DOLORES & EDDIE
GAIETY
DANCE TEAM

1981
month
by
month

JANUARY

S	M	T	W	T	F	S
				1	2	3
4	5	6	7	8	9	10
11	12	13	14	15	16	17
18	19	20	21	22	23	24
25	26	27	28	29	30	31

FEBRUARY

S	M	T	W	T	F	S
1	2	3	4	5	6	7
8	9	10	11	12	13	14
15	16	17	18	19	20	21
22	23	24	25	26	27	28

MARCH

S	M	T	W	T	F	S
1	2	3	4	5	6	7
8	9	10	11	12	13	14
15	16	17	18	19	20	21
22	23	24	25	26	27	28
29	30	31				

APRIL

S	M	T	W	T	F	S
			1	2	3	4
5	6	7	8	9	10	11
12	13	14	15	16	17	18
19	20	21	22	23	24	25
26	27	28	29	30		

MAY

S	M	T	W	T	F	S
					1	2
3	4	5	6	7	8	9
10	11	12	13	14	15	16
17	18	19	20	21	22	23
24	25	26	27	28	29	30
31						

JUNE

S	M	T	W	T	F	S
	1	2	3	4	5	6
7	8	9	10	11	12	13
14	15	16	17	18	19	20
21	22	23	24	25	26	27
28	29	30				

JULY

S	M	T	W	T	F	S
			1	2	3	4
5	6	7	8	9	10	11
12	13	14	15	16	17	18
19	20	21	22	23	24	25
26	27	28	29	30	31	

AUGUST

S	M	T	W	T	F	S
						1
2	3	4	5	6	7	8
9	10	11	12	13	14	15
16	17	18	19	20	21	22
23	24	25	26	27	28	29
30	31					

SEPTEMBER

S	M	T	W	T	F	S
		1	2	3	4	5
6	7	8	9	10	11	12
13	14	15	16	17	18	19
20	21	22	23	24	25	26
27	28	29	30			

OCTOBER

S	M	T	W	T	F	S
				1	2	3
4	5	6	7	8	9	10
11	12	13	14	15	16	17
18	19	20	21	22	23	24
25	26	27	28	29	30	31

NOVEMBER

S	M	T	W	T	F	S
1	2	3	4	5	6	7
8	9	10	11	12	13	14
15	16	17	18	19	20	21
22	23	24	25	26	27	28
29	30					

DECEMBER

S	M	T	W	T	F	S
		1	2	3	4	5
6	7	8	9	10	11	12
13	14	15	16	17	18	19
20	21	22	23	24	25	26
27	28	29	30	31		

THE GIFT (1936)   This is very much a bread-and-butter cover, but by 1936 Rockwell had learned how to present the uninspired with a degree of panache. He has allowed the old man to occupy practically the whole canvas. This gives a concreteness to his presence that would probably have been lacking if this same subject had been painted a dozen years earlier.

DISCOVERING SANTA (1956) As Norman Rockwell's career progressed, it became more and more imperative for him to find new ways of dealing with Christmas. In this painting, a glimmer of realization is apparent in the boy's eyes, but the illusion is not completely shattered. We are permitted to assume that he still believes in Santa, even though he recognizes that the man he saw at the store was not the real thing.

December 1980

22
monday

23
tuesday

24
wednesday

25
thursday — CHRISTMAS

26
friday

27
saturday

28
sunday

December

29
monday _____

30
tuesday _____

31
wednesday _____

January 1981

1
thursday   NEW YEAR'S DAY _____

2
friday _____

3
saturday _____

4
sunday

PARDON ME! (1918)   The clothes sported by these young partygoers place them firmly in their period, but the situation Rockwell pictures here is one that he might just as easily have tackled in the Thirties or the Fifties. A study of Rockwell's early work will, in fact, demonstrate conclusively that he was first and foremost a skillful storyteller.

GARY COOPER (1930) While visiting Hollywood, Rockwell was taken
to the set where Gary Cooper and Fay Wray were at work on *The Texan*,
and here he observed the comical, yet everyday, scene of the he-man
movie star being made up for the camera. His faithful record of this has
to be considered one of his best paintings of the period. His study of the
makeup artist—so far removed from the stereotype—is every bit as interesting as the portrait of the star.

January 1981

5
monday

6
tuesday

7
wednesday

8
thursday

9
friday

10
saturday

11
sunday

January

12
monday _____

13
tuesday _____

14
wednesday _____

15
thursday ___ MARTIN LUTHER KING'S BIRTHDAY _____

16
friday _____

17
saturday _____

18
sunday

WAR NEWS (1945)   Here we are being shown real people in a real setting. There is an intimacy about this group that is totally convincing. We understand the relationship of the three men without having to be told a word of dialogue. We are presented with enough of the interior to know exactly what kind of place it is. From the information we are given it is easy for us to conjure up the rest of the room, other customers, even the kind of neighborhood in which it might be situated.

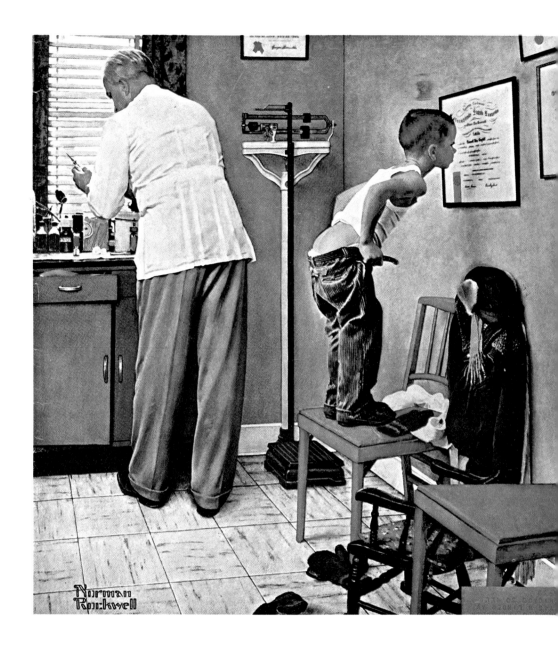

BEFORE THE SHOT (1958) Had Norman Rockwell not been a gifted artist, he might well have become a successful writer or director for films or television. No one has a better knack for inventing comic situations than Rockwell and the ability to create an authentic setting for each incident. All of us have been in rooms like this, and we know that every detail is just right.

January

19
monday _____

20
tuesday _____

21
wednesday _____

22
thursday _____

23
friday _____

24
saturday _____

25
sunday

January

26
monday

27
tuesday

28
wednesday

29
thursday

30
friday

31
saturday

February

1
sunday

ALL BUTTONED UP (1936) We do not see the faces of the young lovers, we do not hear the sweet nothings that he is whispering in her ear, but we do see the reaction that the couple provokes on the features of a rather prim-looking gentleman attempting to lose himself in some inspirational work.

PORTRAIT IN SNOW (1919)   In his early years Norman Rockwell was influenced by shifting editorial policy and by exposure to the work of other artists, but as he assimilated new ideas Rockwell somehow always managed to give them an original twist, making them his own property. A steady growth from the conventional to the unique has been the hallmark of his career.

February

2
monday_____

3
tuesday_____

4
wednesday_____

5
thursday_____

6
friday_____

7
saturday_____

8
sunday

February

9
monday_____

10
tuesday_____

11
wednesday_____

12
thursday_____ LINCOLN'S BIRTHDAY _____

13
friday_____

14
saturday_____ ST. VALENTINE'S DAY _____

15
sunday

JESTER (1939)   This gloomy jester is most notable for the way in which he so completely occupies the page. This painting shows us just how far Rockwell had come from the early days when, faced with the same subject matter, he would have quite simply "floated" the image in the center of the page, leaving it to the *Post's* elegant logo to carry the weight of the design.

THE ARTIST (1938)   There must have been times when even Norman Rockwell's seemingly bottomless well of invention ran dry, and here he amus-
ingly illustrates just such a situation. He is caught at that dreadful moment,
faced with a canvas that is terrifyingly blank except for the familiar *Post*
logo.

February

16
monday_____WASHINGTON'S HOLIDAY_____

17
tuesday_____

18
wednesday_____

19
thursday_____

20
friday_____

21
saturday_____

22
sunday   TRADITIONAL WASHINGTON'S BIRTHDAY

February

23
monday

24
tuesday

25
wednesday

26
thursday

27
friday

28
saturday

March

1
sunday

DOCTOR AND DOLL (1929) This elderly doctor is shown with a nervous child who has just arrived at his office. Her face is clouded with apprehension, but the doctor does his best to set her mind at rest by entering her fantasy world and placing his stethoscope to her doll's chest.

SOUR NOTE (1931) At first this, too, looks like a period cover, but the painting represents not a nineteenth-century military bandsman taking time out from KP, but, rather, a twentieth-century grocer rehearsing for his duties in the local marching band. Judging from the dog's expresson, the trumpeter's abilities are strictly those of the amateur.

March

2
monday _____

3
tuesday _____

4
wednesday _____

5
thursday _____

6
friday _____

7
saturday _____

8
sunday

March

9
monday

10
tuesday

11
wednesday

12
thursday

13
friday

14
saturday

15
sunday

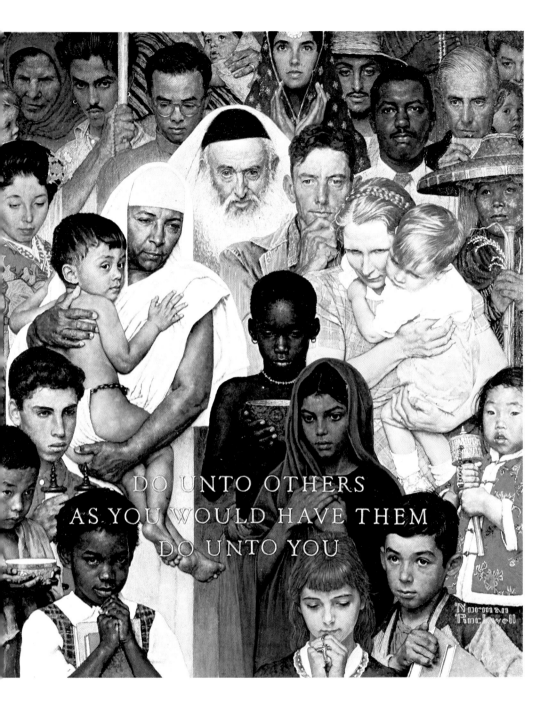

DO UNTO OTHERS
AS YOU WOULD HAVE THEM
DO UNTO YOU

THE GOLDEN RULE (1961) In this painting Norman Rockwell crowded his canvas with a symbolic catalogue of the family of man. Christians and Hindus, Muslims and Jews, Buddhists and Shintoists stand shoulder to shoulder in an heroic composition.

MAN THREADING A NEEDLE (1922) The man's features are a wonderful study in concentration, his tongue held firmly between teeth and lips and his nose pointing the way for the thread to go. When he finishes with the sock he will still not be ready for the comforts of his newspaper and pipe. A button is missing from his vest.

March

16
monday

17
tuesday ST. PATRICK'S DAY

18
wednesday

19
thursday

20
friday

21
saturday

22
sunday

March

23
monday

24
tuesday

25
wednesday

26
thursday

27
friday

28
saturday

29
sunday

THE NATION'S HERO (1919) In this early painting the proud doughboy stands erect, his head held high, surrounded by admiring kids who are reliving his brave deed in their imagination. The redheaded GI in Rockwell's later work (see week May 21-27) is an entirely different concept. The doughboy of 1919 is idealized by the artist. The GI of 1945 is humanized, and this is the measure of Rockwell's growth as an illustrator during the intervening years.

BOULEVARD HAUSSMAN (1932) An attractive young tourist has sought the assistance of a member of the Parisian constabulary. His immensely Gallic gesture seems to suggest that she is demanding too much of his time—or that there is some serious language problem here—and her grip on his cloak indicates that she has no intention of letting him go until he produces the information she needs.

March

30
monday _____

31
tuesday _____

April

1
wednesday _____

2
thursday _____

3
friday _____

4
saturday _____

5
sunday

April

6
monday _____

7
tuesday _____

8
wednesday _____

9
thursday _____

10
friday _____

11
saturday _____

12
sunday

BARBERSHOP QUARTET (1936) Norman Rockwell recalls an era that was almost half a century in the past. We can almost hear their voices as they harmonize some old favorite—"Down by the Old Mill Stream"—and this in turn evokes the clatter of horse-drawn buses and wagons on the cobbled streets outside the barbershop.

EASTER MORNING (1959)   The head of the household does his best to become invisible, but Rockwell's brush misses nothing. The argument is
over, and soon the backslider will be able to enjoy the Sunday sports pages
in peace, but first he must go through this final ritual embarrassment. There
are many ways in which this subject could have been treated, but, as usual,
Rockwell picks exactly the key moment—right down to capturing the son's
envious glance.

April

13
monday

14
tuesday

15
wednesday

16
thursday

17
friday GOOD FRIDAY

18
saturday

19
sunday EASTER

FIRST DAY OF PASSOVER

April

20
monday _____

21
tuesday _____

22
wednesday _____

23
thursday _____

24
friday _____

25
saturday _____

26
sunday

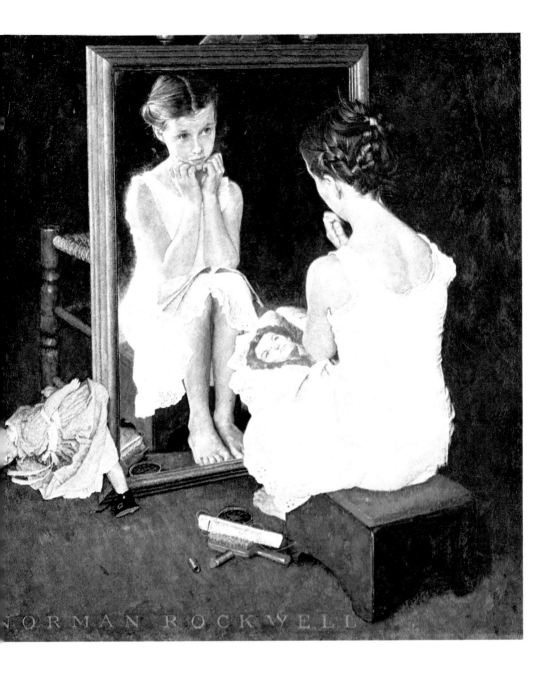

GIRL AT THE MIRROR (1954) In painting this girl studying herself in a mirror, with a movie star's portrait resting on her knees, Rockwell has been completely successful in capturing the poignancy of the moment. The picture has the immediacy of a snapshot and is charged with symbolism— the doll cast aside tells us that that phase of the girl's life is almost over— as she comes to the brink of womanhood.

HOMECOMING GI (1945)   Rather than set the GI's homecoming in some comfortable suburban environment, Norman Rockwell chose to locate it in a big-city tenement area where his mother waits with open arms, and the girl next door who has blossomed during his absence is waiting shyly to be noticed.

April

27
monday _____

28
tuesday _____

29
wednesday _____

30
thursday _____

May

1
friday _____

2
saturday _____

3
sunday

May

4 monday _____

5 tuesday _____

6 wednesday _____

7 thursday _____

8 friday _____

9 saturday _____

10 sunday   MOTHER'S DAY

SAYING GRACE (1951) *Saying Grace* may be the best known of all Norman Rockwell's *Post* covers, and it is not hard to see why it has remained such a great favorite. The idea of the small boy and his grandmother thanking God for their food in a seedy railroad-station cafeteria was custom-made for Rockwell's particular skills in which the environment is superbly evoked.

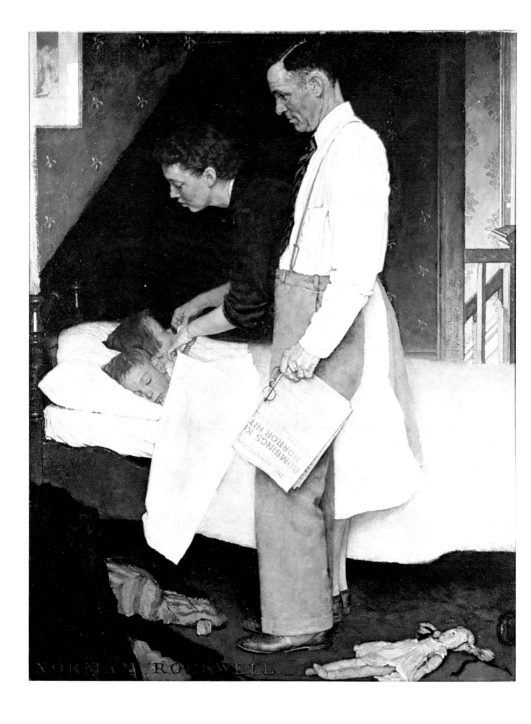

FREEDOM FROM FEAR (1943) This is the most effective and affecting of Rockwell's "Four Freedoms." It is the most ordinary of scenes, and it is this fact that makes the painting so convincing. Rockwell seems to be saying that freedom is most valuable when we can take it for granted.

May

11
monday

12
tuesday

13
wednesday

14
thursday

15
friday　ARMED FORCES DAY

16
saturday

17
sunday

May

18
monday _____

19
tuesday _____

20
wednesday _____

21
thursday _____

22
friday _____

23
saturday _____

24
sunday

GAME CALLED BECAUSE OF RAIN (1949) Norman Rockwell selected the exact moment at which a ball game is brought to a premature conclusion by inclement weather. The Pittsburgh fielders are already in position, waiting for the Dodger batters to come to the plate. The rain is on the Dodgers' side. Rockwell transforms the three umpires into a monumental, though faintly comical, group and at the same time focuses attention on the sky, from which the rain is beginning to fall.

THE FINAL CURTAIN (1937) For more than a decade performers like Dolores and Eddie, Gaiety Dance Team, had been forced to play second fiddle to the movies, and with every year of the Depression their situation had become worse. By 1937 few theaters were providing live shows as a supplement.

May

25
monday ___ MEMORIAL DAY _____

26
tuesday _____

27
wednesday _____

28
thursday _____

29
friday _____

30
saturday _____

31
sunday

June

1
monday

2
tuesday

3
wednesday

4
thursday

5
friday

6
saturday

7
sunday

THE WINDOW WASHER (1960) Rockwell sees the window washer as the hero of this brief encounter, just as the girl's boss—behind his dreary steel desk—is clearly the butt of the joke. Once again Rockwell takes a simple contrast—between the sedentary life and the outdoor life, big-city style—and turns it into a witty and original painting.

THE GOSSIPS (1948) In this *tour de force* Norman Rockwell tells a story about the telling—and retelling—of a story. His subject is nothing less than the spoken word—specifically the transmission of gossip. We never learn the substance of the calumnies that are being passed from neighbor to neighbor, but the reactions of the individuals involved in this cycle convey the message.

June

8
monday

9
tuesday

10
wednesday

11
thursday

12
friday

13
saturday

14
sunday   FLAG DAY

June

15
monday _____

16
tuesday _____

17
wednesday _____

18
thursday _____

19
friday _____

20
saturday _____

21
sunday   FATHER'S DAY

NOT TALL ENOUGH (1917)   When this cover appeared, the United States had just entered the First World War and Rockwell was himself about to join the U. S. Navy with the exalted rank of third-class varnisher and painter. This particular subject may have been suggested to him by the fact that he had been rejected by the Navy, at the time of his initial application, on the ground that he was eight pounds underweight.

AFTER THE PROM (1957) The notion of putting the young couple in a truck stop is a brilliant piece of invention. There is one enigma, though, that everyone must solve to his own satisfaction. The boy is clearly the son of the truck stop's owner—their features are almost identical—but is the girl a very special date, or did the boy take his own sister to the prom? Only Norman Rockwell knows for sure.

June

22
monday _____

23
tuesday _____

24
wednesday _____

25
thursday _____

26
friday _____

27
saturday _____

28
sunday

June

29
monday

30
tuesday

July
1
wednesday

2
thursday

3
friday

4
saturday INDEPENDENCE DAY

5
sunday

THE OUTING (1947) In these upper and lower panels Rockwell manages to tell us so much about the people on this expedition. The vintage of the car and the number of children tells us that this is a family that has known hard times, and so a day trip to Bennington Lake is an important event in their lives.

Norman
Rockwell

HOME DUTY (1916) When Norman Rockwell was in his twenties, he painted two covers and then took the train to *The Saturday Evening Post* in Philadelphia—and was left to wait impatiently until the art editor reappeared to inform him that the magazine was prepared to buy both covers and was ready to commission three more. Rockwell and the *Post* were associated for the next forty-seven years.

July

6
monday _____

7
tuesday _____

8
wednesday _____

9
thursday _____

10
friday _____

11
saturday _____

12
sunday

July

13
monday _____

14
tuesday _____

15
wednesday _____

16
thursday _____

17
friday _____

18
saturday _____

19
sunday

SPORT (1939)   This study of a dogged angler is a fine example of the style Rockwell was perfecting in the late thirties. We still have the shallow space demanded by the old *Post* cover layout, but Rockwell uses it in a novel way, calling on background color to evoke mood and permitting the fisherman and his boat to occupy almost the entire cover. The yellow of the man's slicker and the orange of the bait-can constrast vividly with the neutral colors that dominate the rest of the painting.

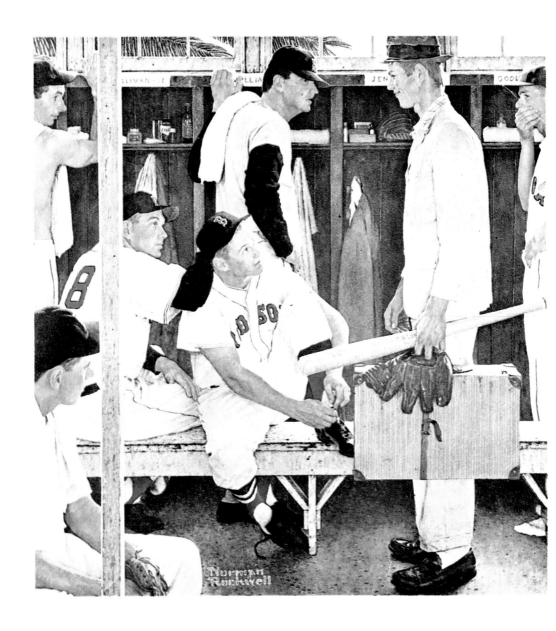

NEW MAN ON THE TEAM (1957) Since Rockwell is, by choice, a New
Englander, it's safe to assume that he is a Red Sox fan, so it was very
natural for him to choose the Boston locker room for this spring-
training cover. All eyes are on the rookie prospect who has just arrived
in camp—all eyes but those of the great Ted Williams, who has, perhaps, seen this all too many times before to allow for much display
of curiosity.

July

20
monday

21
tuesday

22
wednesday

23
thursday

24
friday

25
saturday

26
sunday

July

27
monday_____

28
tuesday_____

29
wednesday_____

30
thursday_____

31
friday_____

August

1
saturday_____

2
sunday

NO SWIMMING (1921) Three boys discover that a "No Swimming" sign means exactly what it says. Throughout Rockwell's work, boys—and girls too—are not better than they ought to be. Like Tom Sawyer and Huck Finn, they have a knack for getting into any kind of mischief that happens to be placed at their disposal.

DINING OUT (1924)   The life of the hobo was, in truth, often brutish and cruel, but it had its romantic side. It was that romantic side of the hobo world that Rockwell painted in this 1924 cover. The picture is not without its ominous edge, however. Fall has arrived. The trees are shedding their leaves, and we realize that this old tramp will soon have to face the hardships of another bitter winter.

August

3
monday

4
tuesday

5
wednesday

6
thursday

7
friday

8
saturday

9
sunday

August

10
monday_____

11
tuesday_____

12
wednesday_____

13
thursday_____

14
friday_____

15
saturday_____

16
sunday

WALKING TO CHURCH (1953) This is Rockwell's tribute to the kind of neighborhood that one of his great contemporaries, Edward Hopper, loved to paint. Rockwell's approach is far more traditional than Hopper's—he paints in a style that was current long before these buildings were erected—but the picture is nonetheless touching for that. There is garbage on the streets, and you can almost smell yesterday's pork chops in the dining room of the Silver Slipper Grill.

THE CHASE (1937)   This again is a rather ''cinematic'' cover, and it seems reasonable to suppose once more that photographs were used in its preparation. The way that the workman is being pulled off balance is what makes the entire composition work.

August

17
monday_____

18
tuesday_____

19
wednesday_____

20
thursday_____

21
friday_____

22
saturday_____

23
sunday

August

24
monday_____

25
tuesday_____

26
wednesday_____

27
thursday_____

28
friday_____

29
saturday_____

30
sunday

HOME FROM VACATION (1930) This painting of an exhausted young family has all the elements that we associate with Rockwell's maturity as an illustrator. We sense a total confidence in the way he has handled the subject. He knows exactly what must be done to make the situation believable, and he does it with a minimum of fuss.

FIXING A FLAT (1946) We can assume that the two young ladies are off in search of picturesque scenes and instead find themselves stranded beside a rustic eyesore. The weather is threatening, and the hillbilly who studies them from his tottering porch clearly has little regard for the romantic qualities of this mountain landscape.

August

31
monday _____

September

1
tuesday _____

2
wednesday _____

3
thursday _____

4
friday _____

5
saturday _____

6
sunday

September

7
monday _____ LABOR DAY _____

8
tuesday _____

9
wednesday _____

10
thursday _____

11
friday _____

12
saturday _____

13
sunday

A TIME FOR GREATNESS (1964) In his portrayal of the Democratic National Convention, Norman Rockwell created a careful, studied composition, using the standards of a half a dozen states to frame the President-to-be. Instead of trying to compete with the spontaneity of photojournalism, he gives us a symbolic record of the event.

LEAPFROG (1919) It's extraordinary that Rockwell was able to come up with so many lively compositions, given the limitations at the time. The subject matter of this 1919 example, for instance, could hardly be more simple and straightforward, but Rockwell managed to pep it up by using a time-honored trick of the trade, making it seem that the leapfrogging boy is almost literally jumping off the page.

September

14
monday

15
tuesday

16
wednesday

17
thursday

18
friday

19
saturday

20
sunday

September

21
monday_____

22
tuesday_____

23
wednesday_____

24
thursday_____

25
friday_____

26
saturday_____

27
sunday

SPEED TRAP (1929)   Speed traps, as is evident from this picture, were already one of the hazards of motoring in the twenties. This menacing-looking law officer lies in wait behind a sign that bears a message contradicting his intentions. Rockwell's skill, as both painter and story teller, enables us to intuit from this one vignette the character and ambience of Elmville.

GOING OUT (1933)   The device of placing figures with their backs to the viewer is one that Rockwell used frequently and, in this instance, he creates a sense of ambiguity. At other times the pose leaves no doubt as to what we could see if the figure were facing us.

September

28
monday

29
tuesday — ROSH HASHANAH

30
wednesday

October

1
thursday

2
friday

3
saturday

4
sunday

October

5
monday _____

6
tuesday _____

7
wednesday _____

8
thursday _____ YOM KIPPUR _____

9
friday _____

10
saturday _____

11
sunday

CHECKUP (1957) The girl in the center of the composition may have already experienced the ecstasy that her friend is now enjoying, but the other observer, off to the left, is the picture of envy. She cannot wait to acquire the same badge of maturity.

DOUBLE TAKE (1941)   This painting is, quite simply, a visual pun, and it works remarkably well. We look twice before we realize that we are seeing the face of a glamorous, mature woman superimposed—by chance—onto the body of a young co-ed. One reason why it does work (and why it must have been doubly effective during its newsstand life) is that Rockwell has handled it in such an off-handed manner, so that we are deceived by the casualness of the composition and caught off guard.

October

12
monday COLUMBUS DAY

13
tuesday

14
wednesday

15
thursday

16
friday

17
saturday

18
sunday

October

19
monday_____

20
tuesday_____

21
wednesday_____

22
thursday_____

23
friday_____

24
saturday_____

25
sunday

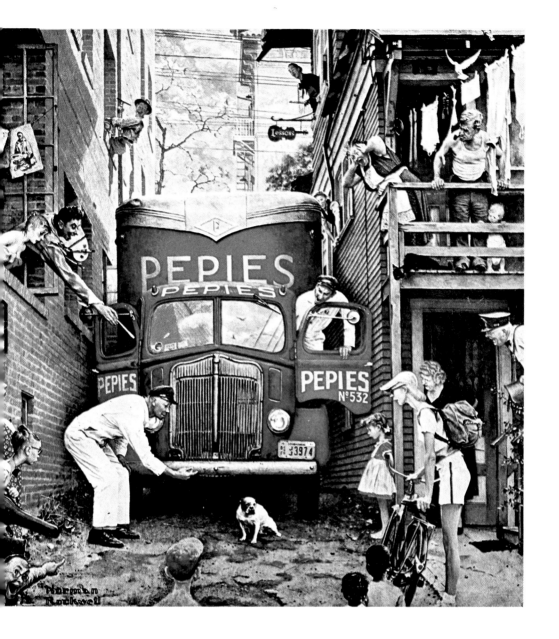

TRAFFIC CONDITIONS (1949)   This painting is packed with colorful characters. There are no fewer than twenty figures not counting the truculent bulldog that is the center of all attention. A truck is blocking a narrow alleyway and its progress made impossible. The incident gives Rockwell the opportunity to evoke lovingly a slightly run-down neighborhood and the people who inhabit it.

FREEDOM OF SPEECH (1943) At the annual town meeting a young blue-collar worker stands up to state his views. Rockwell's viewpoint—that anyone and everyone can have a voice in American politics—is conveyed directly and succinctly.

October

26
monday

27
tuesday

28
wednesday

29
thursday

30
friday

31
saturday HALLOWEEN

November

1
sunday

November

2
monday _____

3
tuesday _____ ELECTION DAY _____

4
wednesday _____

5
thursday _____

6
friday _____

7
saturday _____

8
sunday

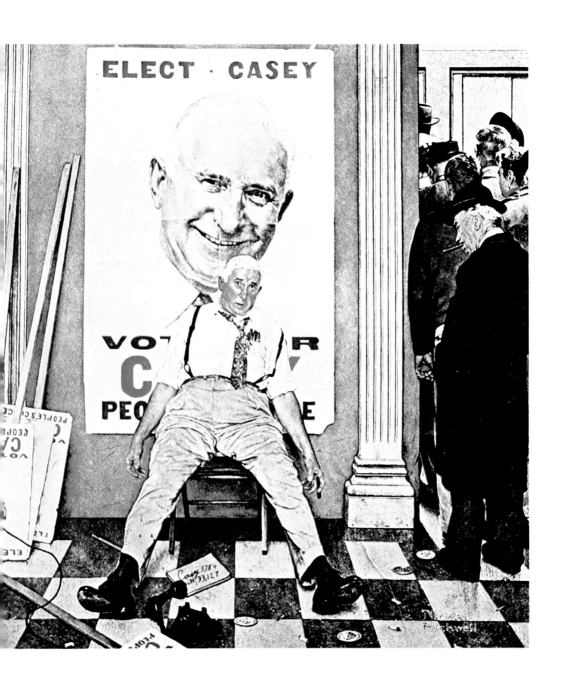

BEFORE AND AFTER (1958)   This man—apparently a candidate for some local office—is caught in the moment of defeat, he is in a state of shock and his hopes are as dead as the cigar that dangles from his fingers. Supporters are filing from the room, leaving the candidate alone with his thoughts.

LOOKING OUT TO SEA (1919) In this early painting Norman Rockwell
has not yet found a personal viewpoint. The technical skill is there, but
in his maturity he would have endowed the old man and the boy with
more character through the trenchant details that are so telling in Rockwell's
later work.

November

9
monday_____

10
tuesday_____

11
wednesday_____ VETERAN'S DAY _____

12
thursday_____

13
friday_____

14
saturday_____

15
sunday

November

16
monday_____

17
tuesday_____

18
wednesday_____

19
thursday_____

20
friday_____

21
saturday_____

22
sunday

THE CONNOISSEUR (1962)   Judging by his dapper clothing and his self-assured pose, we can reasonably assume that the man sees himself as a person of some discernment—yet we cannot imagine that he has any concept of what the artist has put himself through to produce this painting, whether it is good or bad. Rockwell is poking fun at people who set themselves up in judgment of others.

THANKSGIVING (1945) Often we are able to guess at the dialogue that might accompany an incident that Norman Rockwell has painted. In this instance the emotions that have welled up in both mother and son take them beyond words. Just being together in the same room is all the communication that is needed. At the time it first appeared its emotional impact must have been tremendous.

November

23
monday

24
tuesday

25
wednesday

26
thursday   THANKSGIVING

27
friday

28
saturday

29
sunday

November

30
monday _____

December
1
tuesday _____

2
wednesday _____

3
thursday _____

4
friday _____

5
saturday _____

6
sunday

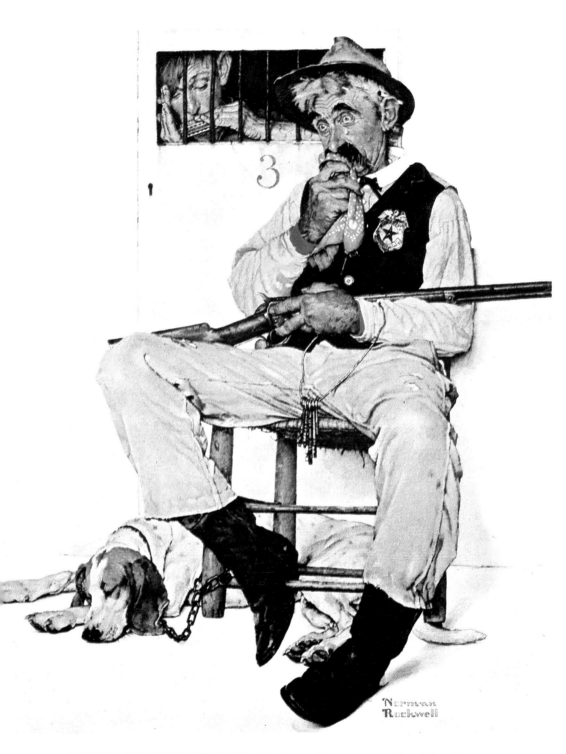

SHERIFF AND PRISONER (1939)   Again we have an example of the sheer skill Rockwell had acquired in the art of designing a magazine cover. The barred window in the cell door has been place as if to punch a hole through the *Post's* logo. This produces the illusion that the prisoner is incarcerated within the magazine itself.

FIRST LOVE (1926) An interesting aspect of this painting is that the two figures are treated quite naturalistically but *appear* to be caricatured because of the clothes they are wearing. The boy's high-waisted trousers and the girl's over-sized shoes alter the proportions of their bodies and add pathos to the scene. Even the sagging bench contributes to the overall mood of the picture.

December

7
monday_____

8
tuesday_____

9
wednesday_____

10
thursday_____

11
friday_____

12
saturday_____

13
sunday

December

14
monday_____

15
tuesday_____

16
wednesday_____

17
thursday_____

18
friday_____

19
saturday_____

20
sunday

FEEDING TIME (1954) More thought has gone into this humorous cover than is, perhaps, apparent at first glance. For example, a less imaginative artist might not have thought of placing the keeper's feet up on the metal guardrail, a device which—because of the foreshortening involved—gives the painting depth and helps draw us into the image.

CHRISTMAS TRIO (1923) In this blatantly Dickensian painting, the man at the left of the group might be Mr. Pickwick himself. The boy is clearly a cousin of Oliver Twist, and it is not difficult to imagine Scrooge confronting the Ghost of Christmas Past in any of the buildings that form the background.

December

21
monday___HANUKKAH_____

22
tuesday_____

23
wednesday_____

24
thursday_____

25
friday___CHRISTMAS_____

26
saturday_____

27
sunday

December

28
monday

29
tuesday

30
wednesday

31
thursday

January 1982

1
friday   NEW YEAR'S DAY

2
saturday

3
sunday

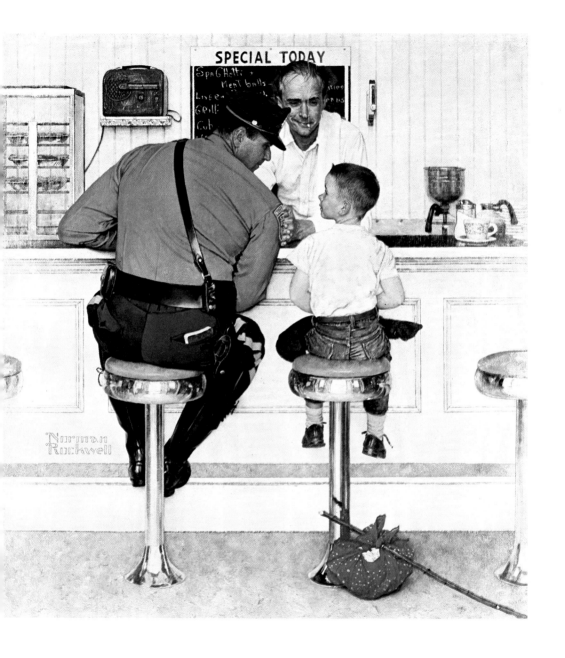

THE RUNAWAY (1958) The state trooper, like the short-order cook behind the counter, is clearly in sympathy with this boy's dream of a life on the open road. The cop's broad shoulders, uniform and sidearm are set off against the boy's slender physique, white tee shirt and pathetic travel kit.

FREEDOM FROM WANT (1943) In this painting, Rockwell used every visual device available to him—from the happy expression on the faces of the gathered family at Thanksgiving to the sunlight gleaming on the china —to convey the full meaning of "Freedom from Want."

January

4
monday_____

5
tuesday_____

6
wednesday_____

7
thursday_____

8
friday_____

9
saturday_____

10
sunday

January

11
monday

12
tuesday

13
wednesday

14
thursday

15
friday — MARTIN LUTHER KING'S BIRTHDAY

16
saturday

17
sunday

ABBEVILLE PRESS, INC. • 505 Park Avenue, New York 10022

Printed in the U.S.A.

ISBN 0-89659-109-3